"This is dedicated to my niece Hayley who provided personal insight into a child's perspective of Type I Diabetes having developed the condition at 7 years old. Also to Emma Greenaway and Harriet Broome who also developed diabetes at 5yrs old."

ISBN: 978-0-9931014-1-0

Susie Sugar and Tom.

Written by Heather Hawley
Illustrated by Sarah-Leigh Wills

CHAPTER 1

Tom

Tom is a seven year old boy who likes nothing better than playing outdoors, riding his bike and kicking a ball around with his friend Robert. At school he loves PE lessons and, in particular, the summer sports days when he teams up with Robert to do the Three Legged Race. His Mum struggles to keep Tom supplied with food at times; he always seems to be saying:

'I'm hungry Mum, what is there to eat?' He starts his day with a big bowl of cereal, a glass of orange juice, and if he has time, two pieces of toast. 'Don't forget to brush your teeth,' says his Mum as he leaves the table. Mid-morning he has a snack of fruit and at lunchtime he devours everything his Mum has put in his lunch box. As soon as he gets home from school he starts again. 'What's for tea Mum, I'm hungry!'

Although Tom is eating lots of food, he never gets fat because it is all used to make the energy he needs to run around and play games. Time passes quickly for Tom and before he knows it his Mum is calling him: 'Come on Tom, clean your teeth and jump into bed.'

Mum reads him a bedtime story, but he doesn't hear much of it as he is so tired from running around during the day.

He quickly falls asleep.

Coming home from school one day Tom moans to Mum: 'I feel tired!'

Although he has been playing at school all day as usual, now home, he just sits quietly.

'Don't you want to go out to play Tom?' says his Mum.

'No,' says Tom sullenly, 'I'll just practice my reading.' This surprises Mum as he would usually be wriggling and bouncing around wanting to go out! The next morning Tom says crabbily: 'I don't want to get out of bed Mum!'

She checks him over but couldn't find anything wrong, so decides to send him to school. In school Tom cannot be bothered to do any work. His teacher, Miss Pigglebottom, asks him to pick up all the pencils after the morning lessons. 'I'm too tired,' he grumbles 'Why can't Robert do it instead?'

Later in the day Tom refuses to sit by Miss Pigglebottom to do his reading. He keeps asking to go to the toilet. Miss Pigglebottom was getting quite cross with him until she wonders whether he might be feeling unwell.

Tom cannot be bothered with anything.
'Are you coming out to play football, Tom?' says Robert.

Tom is rude to him and makes him cry.

Miss Pigglebottom mentions the problems to Mum when she picks him up from school. 'Oh dear,' Mum says, concerned 'He didn't seem very happy this morning.'

When they got home Tom eats some tea and Mum sends him to bed early. During the night Tom wakes up feeling very thirsty. He goes to the bathroom to get a glass of water.

In the morning Mum calls: 'Tom, time to get up!'

'Oh no,' exclaims Tom 'I've peed my pants!'

He quickly puts on dry ones and runs downstairs to tell his Mum. He looks quite sad.

'Mum, I feel a bit sick and I have a tummy ache.' Whilst he sits at the breakfast table eating his cereal, he looks quite miserable.

Mum decides he should stay home from school and have a quiet day. Tom nibbles on bits of food and has lots to drink.

'Best go to bed early tonight Tom. If you are no better in the morning I think I should take you to the doctors,' says Mum.

Tom really didn't care.
He gulps down a big glass of water and quickly falls asleep.
He wakes up in the night and yet again needs a drink.
In the morning Tom feels something wet. 'Oh no, I've wet the bed, what on earth is happening to me?'

CHAPTER 2

Susie Sugar

In the meantime, things have been going on inside Tom's body. The cereals he had eaten for breakfast contained some sugar – Susie Sugar. Susie was filled with excitement when she had at last fallen out of the cereal packet and into Tom's bowl, tumbling along with all the other bits. When Tom poured on the milk she exclaimed 'Goodness gracious, what was that, I'm all wet?!' But there was no time to ponder because Tom's spoon plunges Susie and some other bits of cereal into the dark cavern of his mouth. His f l a t wobbly tongue pushes her backwards. With a LARGE swallow from Tom, Susie zooms down the food pipe and lands with a

into the vast yellow pool of his stomach! 'Wow,' yells Susie to all the other bits, 'This is great fun!'

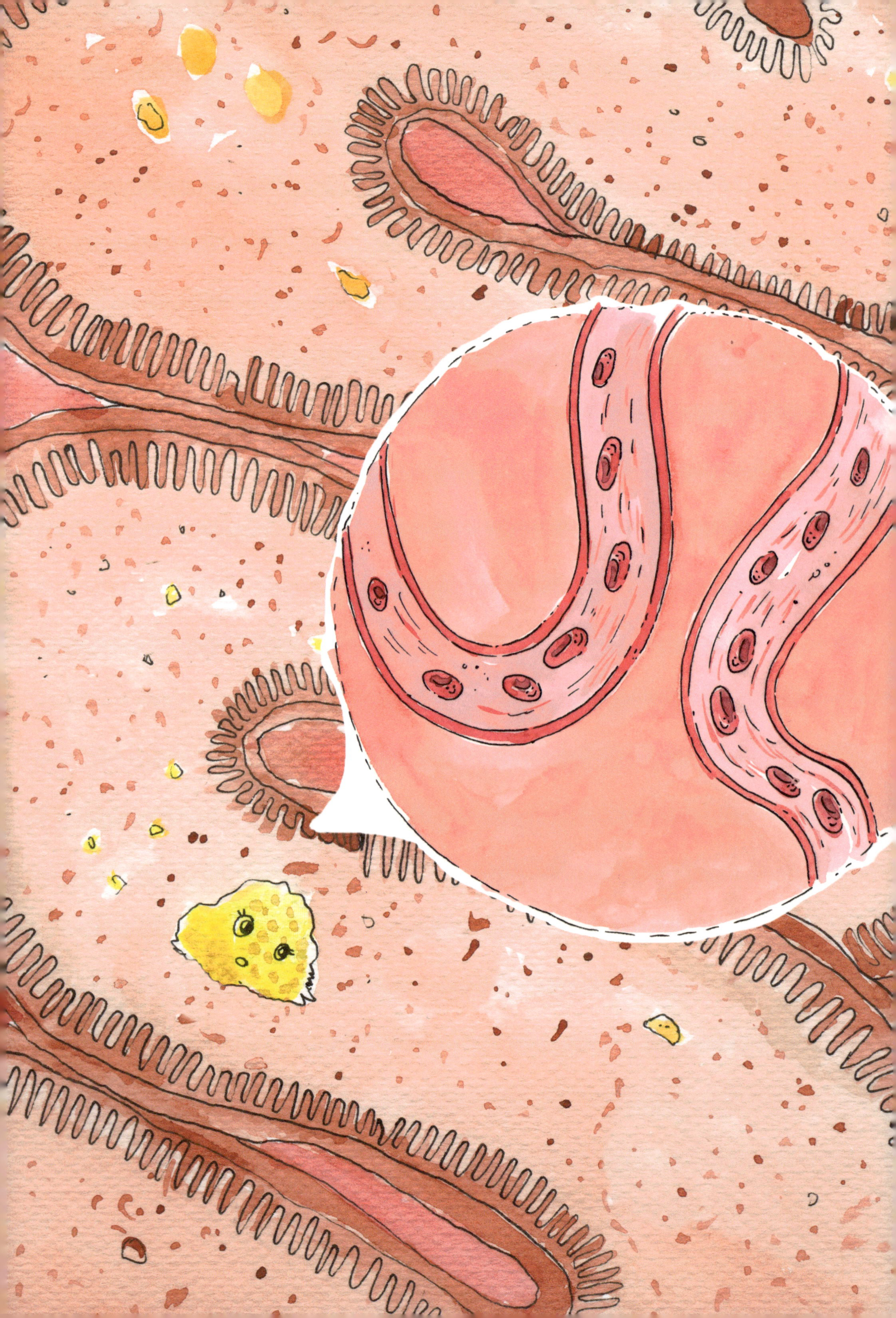

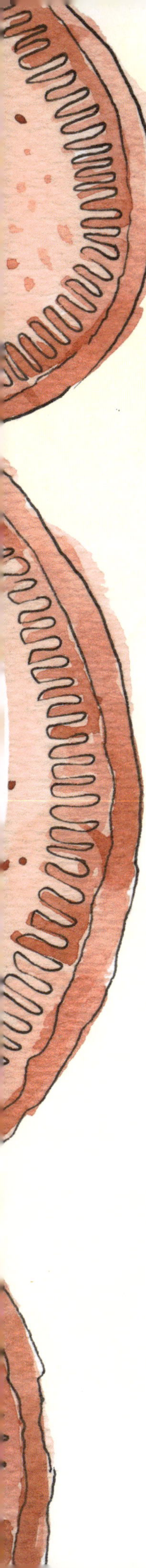

In no time at all there is a quick SQUIRT and Susie finds herself in a long, bending tube. It is the SMALL intestine, which sits inside Tom's tummy. She comes across some things that look like tiny fingers. 'Hello' she says, 'who are you?' They seem very friendly. 'We are the villi. We move food along the small intestine.' It feels like waves as she is gently passed from one villus to the next. 'Mmmm,' thinks Susie, 'this is very relaxing.' What Susie hasn't realised is that while she is enjoying the ride through the SMALL intestine, she changes from sugar into glucose. Now she is Susie Glucose not Susie Sugar!

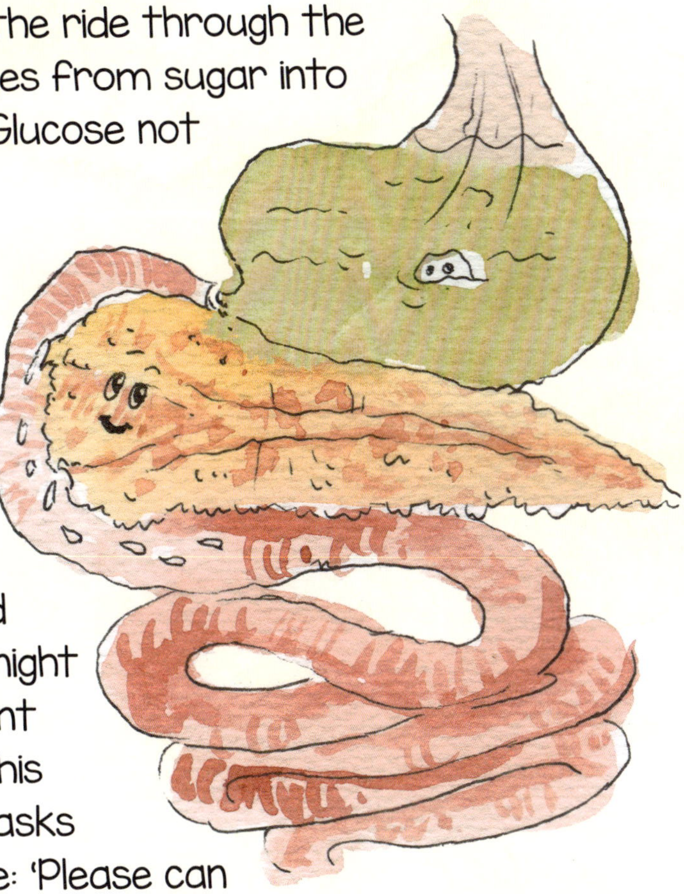

Running along through thin, elastic tubes within the villi is some red liquid known as blood; Brucey Blood. Through these tubes, known as blood vessels, he travels around the inside of Tom's body night and day carrying important things from one part of his body to another. Brucey asks Susie Glucose, with a smile: 'Please can I use you to make energy for Tom?' 'No you certainly can't. I am quite happy here with the soft friendly villi thank you very much!' Brucey is used to this response from the food he meets so continues, with a chuckle: 'You are very important Susie.' Susie beamed: she liked the sound of this. 'Now you have been changed into glucose Tom can use you for energy. He needs lots of this because he spends so much time racing around and playing football with Robert.' Susie feels very proud to be so important. 'OK,' she says. She slips through the wall of the small intestine and is whisked away with Brucey!

Brucey Blood rushes along. Susie notices he has something else with him. 'What's that other stuff coming along with us?' she says. 'Well,' frowns Brucey 'that's insulin. I visit lots of places in Tom's body, one of them is called 'the pancreas.' It is a l o n g, f l a t, blobby thing with a special part called Islets of Langerhan, which sorts out insulin for me. I need insulin when I am carrying a lot of glucose like you Susie.'

Susie starts to feel a bit lost with all this information. 'I thought that it would be just ME with you Brucey - not all this OTHER stuff as well!'

'Well, I'm sure you will learn to like insulin Susie. Insulin helps me put glucose into the right place in Tom's body. You see, insulin is a hormone. There are various hormones in the body and they work like keys, opening doors to different functions.'

Susie is not feeling very convinced about any of it.

Insulin, in the meantime, is very busy opening CELLS. They are tiny and can only be seen through a microscope. As soon as insulin unlocks the CELLS, all the glucose like Susie can get inside them.

'It's like this Susie,' Brucey tries to explain further, 'I carry you and your other glucose friends to the CELLS in Toms body. When you arrive, insulin opens the CELL for you. After you get into the CELL you can be used for energy. If we didn't do this for him, he wouldn't have any strength to run around or even just sit and play on his computer. Also, lots of other parts of his body wouldn't work properly.'

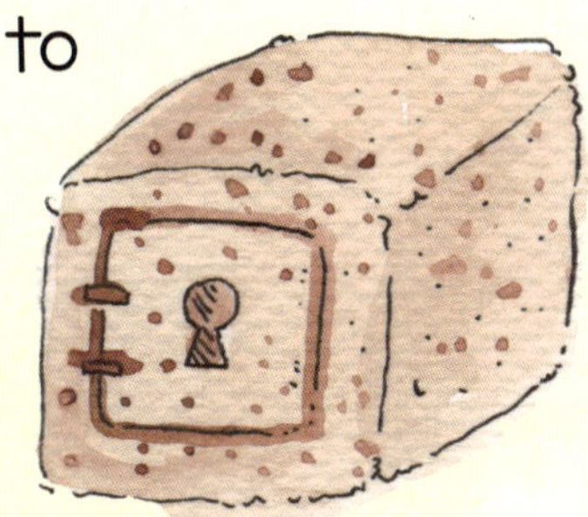

Susie liked the sound of this so Brucey whisked her away along the blood vessels to another part of Tom.

When Brucey drops her off at a CELL Susie waits and waits in anticipation. More glucose comes along. She starts to get fed up. 'When is that special insulin going to come along and unlock a CELL for me?' she thinks. There is no insulin to be seen. Poor Susie! She thinks perhaps she is not good enough for Tom.

Brucey Blood becomes very worried, 'Oh dear, what can be happening? Where is the insulin? What am I to do with all this glucose? How am I going to get it into the cells?'

CHAPTER 3

Tom Becomes Unwell...

Tom's body is now getting littered with too much glucose from the food he has eaten during the day.

When the body gets like this, it tries to get rid of the glucose in other ways: one way is by putting some of it into your pee. This is what was happening inside Tom's body. 'Oh my word' grumbles Brucey when he realises what is happening 'Now I need to supply some extra fluid to help water down the glucose in Tom's pee!' Because Brucey is using up extra water for pee, this makes Tom feel thirsty. He drinks a lot more, and then he needs to use the toilet more often. 'I know why I need to pee so much,' sighs Tom, 'because for some reason I want to drink lots of water. That's why I wet the bed in my sleep.' Poor Tom. He struggles to make sense of it all. Even though he has eaten he still feels weak. Susie Glucose and friends are still being made from Tom's food, but it cannot be used as there is no insulin coming along to unlock the CELLS. If Susie cannot get into a CELL Tom will not be able to use her for energy!

Although Tom ate all his breakfast he doesn't feel very well.
'I feel sick and my tummy hurts Mum,' he groans. 'I feel hot and tired.'

His Mum telephones the school to speak to Miss Pigglebottom.
'Tom will not be coming into school today, he's still not well,' Mum says.

Robert is upset when he hears the news. 'I have bought a new toy tractor and want to show it to Tom!'

Tom's Mum phones the Doctor's surgery. She is given an appointment with the Nurse Practitioner for later that day. Tom has some drinks and sleeps most of the morning. When it is time to go to the surgery Mum picks him up and carries him to the car. 'That's funny,' she thinks, 'his breath smells strange. It's almost fruity like pear drops, but he hasn't had anything fruity today!'

Inside Tom, Susie Glucose and her friends are fed up.

'What's happening?' they quiz Brucey Blood, 'why aren't the CELLS being unlocked?'

Brucey is fed up too.
'How can I do my job properly if insulin doesn't come along to unlock the CELLS?'

Brucey goes to see pancreas.
A very glum Pancreas says:
'For some reason Brucey I cannot make insulin for Tom. This makes me feel very sad because if I can't make insulin, Tom will become ill. I don't know what to do!'

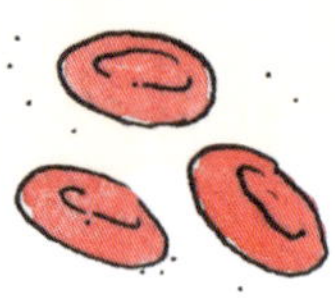

CHAPTER 4

Going to the Surgery...

Mum and Tom arrive at the surgery. They tell the Nurse what has been happening. 'Tom, can you spend a penny for me?' says the Nurse. Tom looks confused and thinks: 'that's weird. Why do I need to spend a penny and where do I get the penny from?'

Realising he doesn't understand, the nurse asks Mum: 'can you get him to pass some urine into a bottle for me to test please?'

'What is urine?' says Tom.

'It's another name for pee, Tom.'

'Oh! Well, that is NO problem! All I seem to do all day is drink and pee!' The nurse smiles. 'Can I prick your finger Tom to get a bit of blood?' Tom isn't too sure about this, he thinks it might hurt. 'I will do it very quickly, Tom. It will help me work out what is wrong with you.'

Tom looks away but holds out his finger for her. A quick prick and it is done. 'Oh, that wasn't so bad!' says Tom.

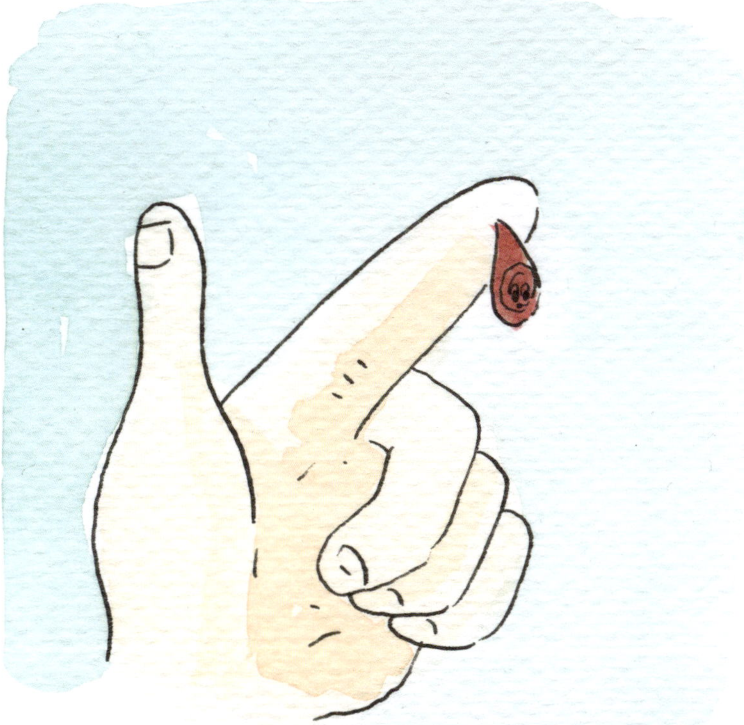 

After testing his pee and blood the Nurse sits back down with Tom and his Mum. 'I think Tom has Type I Diabetes,' says the Nurse. Mum is upset. She thought that Tom was just messing about but now she realises he has been feeling quite poorly. She is pleased that a reason has been found so that Tom can get back to normal quite soon. 'Don't worry,' say's the nurse kindly. 'The symptoms aren't always obvious.' The Nurse telephones the hospital and speaks to the special Doctor who looks after children. 'Can Tom's Mum bring him here straight away?' says the Doctor.

The nurse asks Mum, who replies: 'Of course. Whatever it takes to make Tom better!' While Mum drives him to the hospital, Tom spies a tube of sweets in the car. 'Can I eat these sweets please Mum?' he asks with a big grin on his face.

'No Tom. I'm sorry but they have lots of sugar in them which will make you worse. I will give them to Robert.' This made Tom cross; he didn't like the sound of this adventure at all.

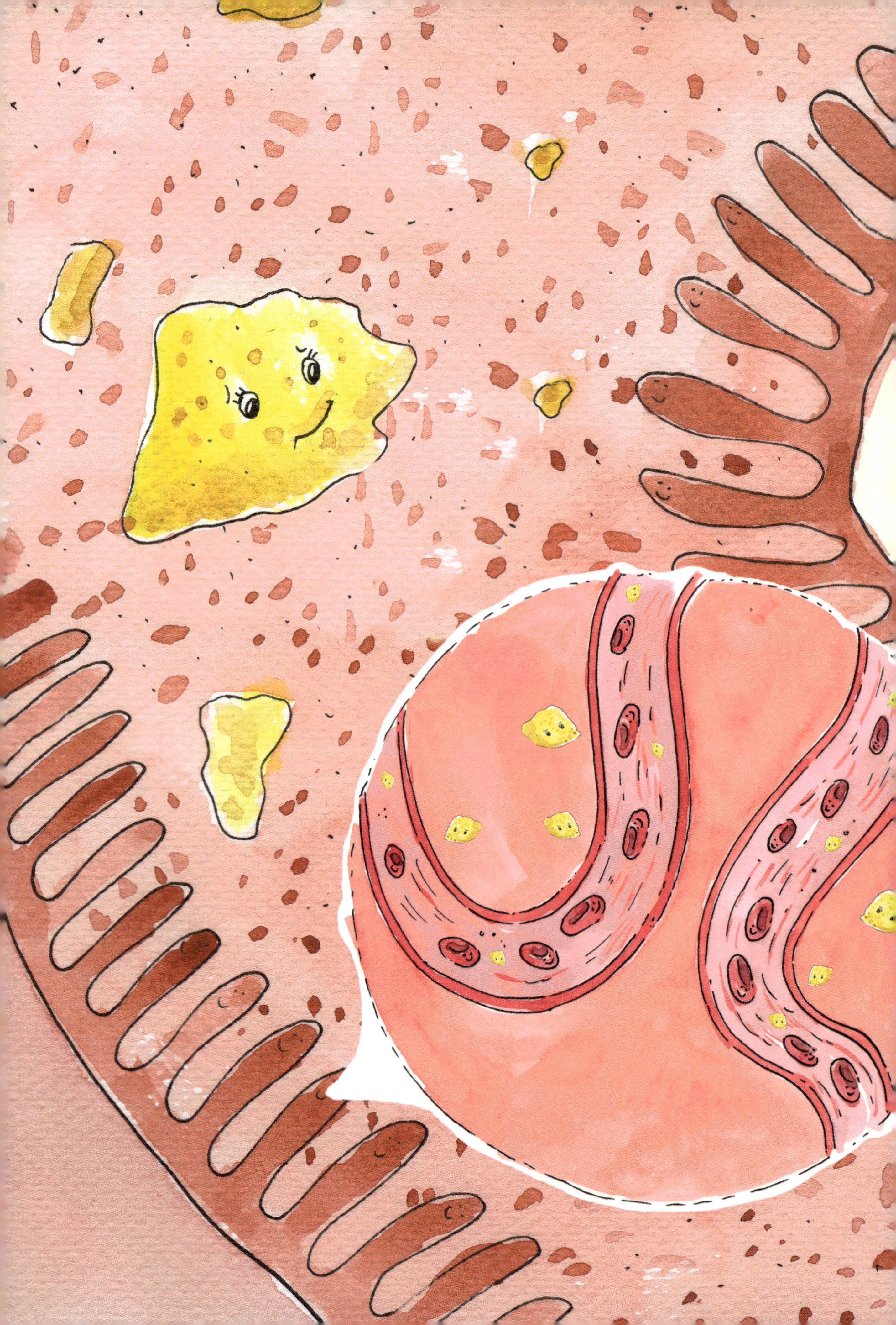

Inside Tom, Brucey Blood is busy doing all his other jobs. Usually he is whizzing around carrying all the things Tom needs to keep him healthy and getting rid of the things his body doesn't need. All this is going on whether Tom is awake and playing with Robert, or at night when he is asleep. Now everything is different.

'I'm not moving around very fast today,' thinks Brucey. 'I think Tom has spent a lot of time sitting around. I feel all thick and sticky because I'm having to put so much water into Tom's pee!' Tom's arms and legs feel weak because there is no insulin to open the CELLS for Susie Glucose and her friends, so his energy levels are getting very low. Usually Susie Glucose and her friends would be in the CELLS, looking forward to giving Tom power in his muscles. 'How can I put energy into Tom's muscles and make him feel stronger if insulin doesn't unlock the CELLS for Susie and her friends?' grumbles Brucey. 'It's no good, we will just have to use some of Tom's fat.'

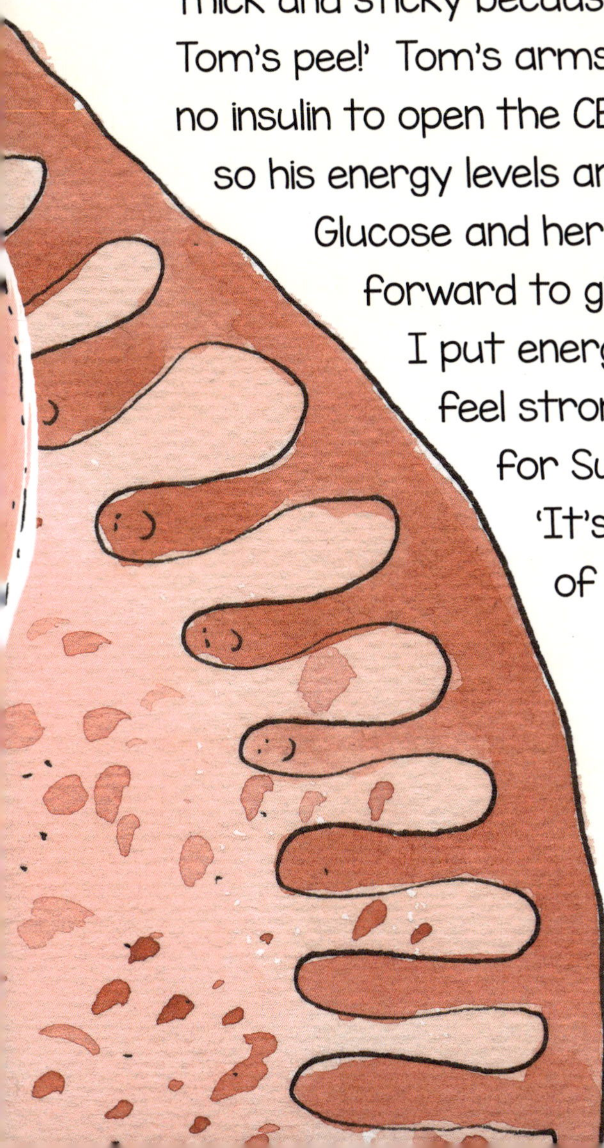

When the body uses fat for energy instead of Susie Glucose and her friends, it makes something called ketones. When ketones are in your blood it makes your breath smell fruity. This is what Mum could smell when she put Tom in the car.

The ketones were also in Tom's pee along with some friends of Susie Glucose. When the nurse did the special tests on Tom's pee and Brucey Blood she found they contained lots of ketones and glucose. This was how she knew that Tom had diabetes.

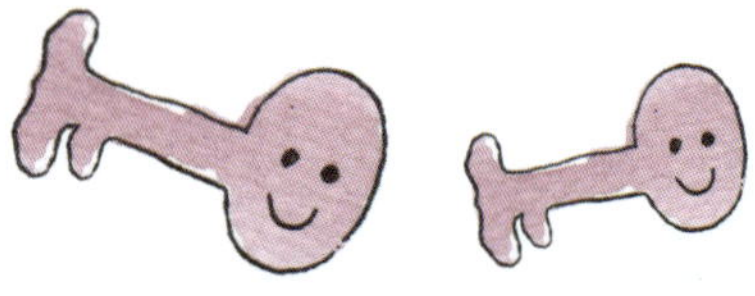

TEST RESULTS:
KETONES

CHAPTER 5

At the Hospital

At the hospital the doctors come and have a chat with Tom and his Mum.

'We need to take some blood from your arm, Tom, then put it in a few of these different coloured bottles.' Tom feels frightened.

'What, with a needle?' he cries!

'Look Tom,' says the kind doctor with a smile,

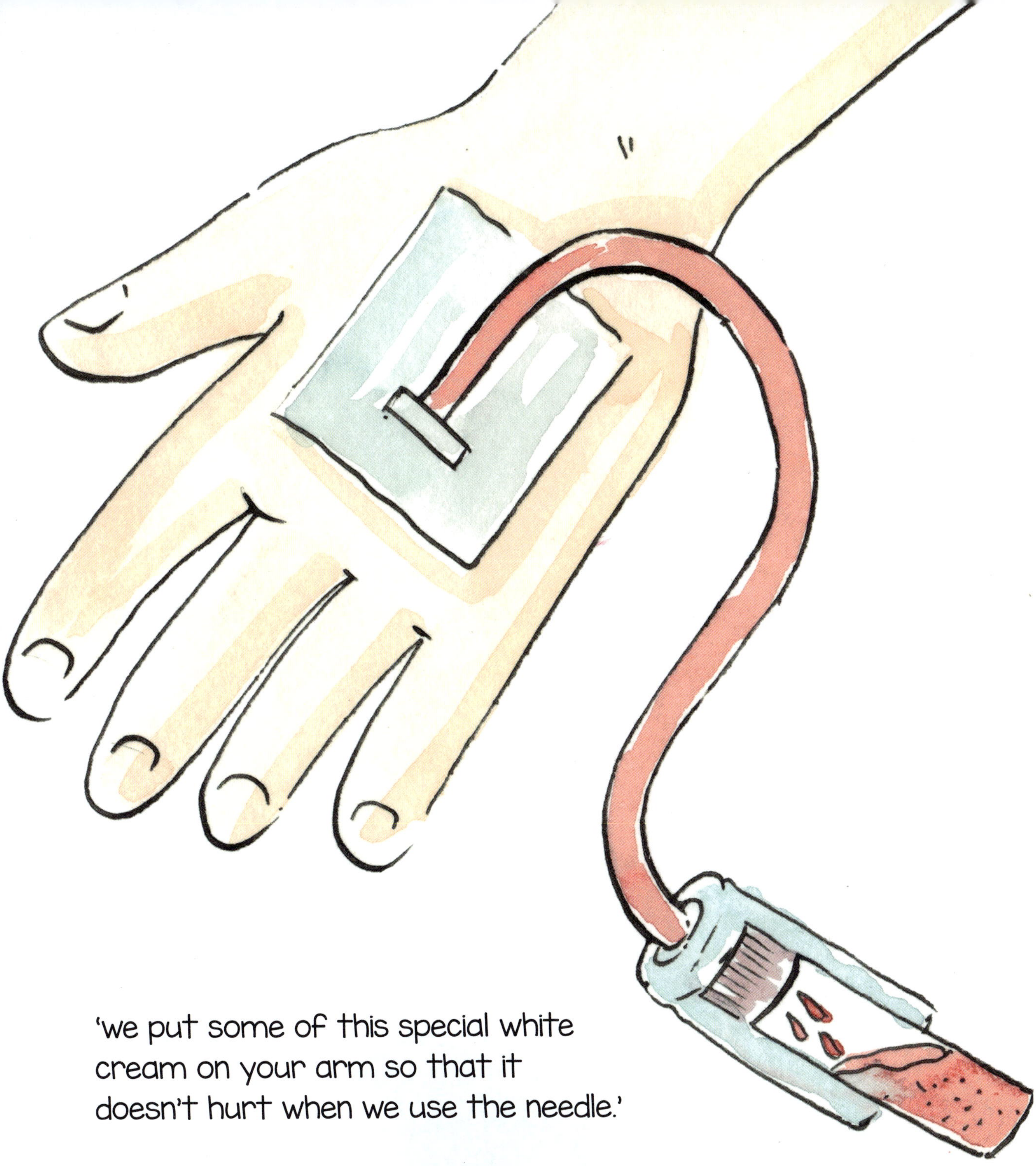

'we put some of this special white cream on your arm so that it doesn't hurt when we use the needle.'

'Oh, OK,' says Tom warily. He was feeling so unwell he didn't really care anymore. They quickly take some blood. 'That didn't hurt at all!' says Tom with a look of surprise. The bottles are taken off to a special place called a laboratory where Brucey Blood is tested to find out what is wrong with Tom. Once they have the results the Doctors can decide what treatment they can give him to make him feel better.

After a short time the doctors come back to see Tom and his Mum. 'It looks like Tom definitely has Type 1 Diabetes' says the doctor.

'What do you mean by THAT?' says Tom, who is now starting to feel really fed up. The doctor does his best to explain. 'This means that a special organ in your body, called a pancreas, cannot make an important liquid called insulin anymore.'

'Can we buy a new pancreas then?'
'No,' chuckles the doctor, 'I wish it was that easy Tom!'
'We will need to give you insulin in another way. It will take a few days for us to get you feeling better so you need to come to our Children's Ward.'

Tom feels scared.

'I have to go somewhere else? Why can't I go home?'
He starts to cry. Mum gives him a cuddle.

'It will be OK Tom. A hospital ward is where people stay when they need special things done to them to make them better. I will stay with you so you won't be alone.'

Once on the ward he realises there is no need to worry. It is a bright, happy place with lots of colourful paintings on the walls and many toys to play with. He meets lots of cheerful nurses and doctors who are very kind and gentle.

0,02

They take the time to tell him what is going to happen. He has a lot more finger pricks. The insulin is given to him via a special pump and a tiny tube that is inserted just under his skin and taped in place.

'I wish I was back playing with Robert and everything was normal again,' Tom sobs!

Mum gives him a hug. 'Now you are being given insulin through that tube Tom, you will soon feel much better. Then you will be able to go home. I know it seems scary now but you will soon get used to everything like lots of the other boys and girls who have Type 1 Diabetes.' She gives him a tickle which makes him laugh and feel a bit better.

Tom plays with the toys on the ward. A cheerful nurse comes along and says: 'Come on Tom, let's check that your insulin is working OK.' He only has to sit still for a few seconds then is back playing with the toys. He realises he is starting to feel much better.

Now that Tom has some insulin again, to unlock the CELLS, Susie is delighted. 'Great! Now I can get into a CELL!' Brucey is very happy because now Tom has insulin again it can deal with all the glucose that has piled up.

'I can whizz around doing my jobs properly for Tom again!' says Brucey. He meets up with pancreas, who is looking miserable.

'What's wrong pancreas? Why are you looking so glum?'
'I have really let Tom down. He is having to have insulin through a tiny tube because I cannot make it any more,' says pancreas.
'Well don't forget you still have another very important job to do for Tom,' says Brucey, doing his best to be cheerful. 'Have you forgotten that you make special juices to help Tom break down his food in the SMALL intestine?'
'Oh yes! You're right Brucey. I had forgotten. That IS important to keep Tom healthy.' Pancreas feels much happier.

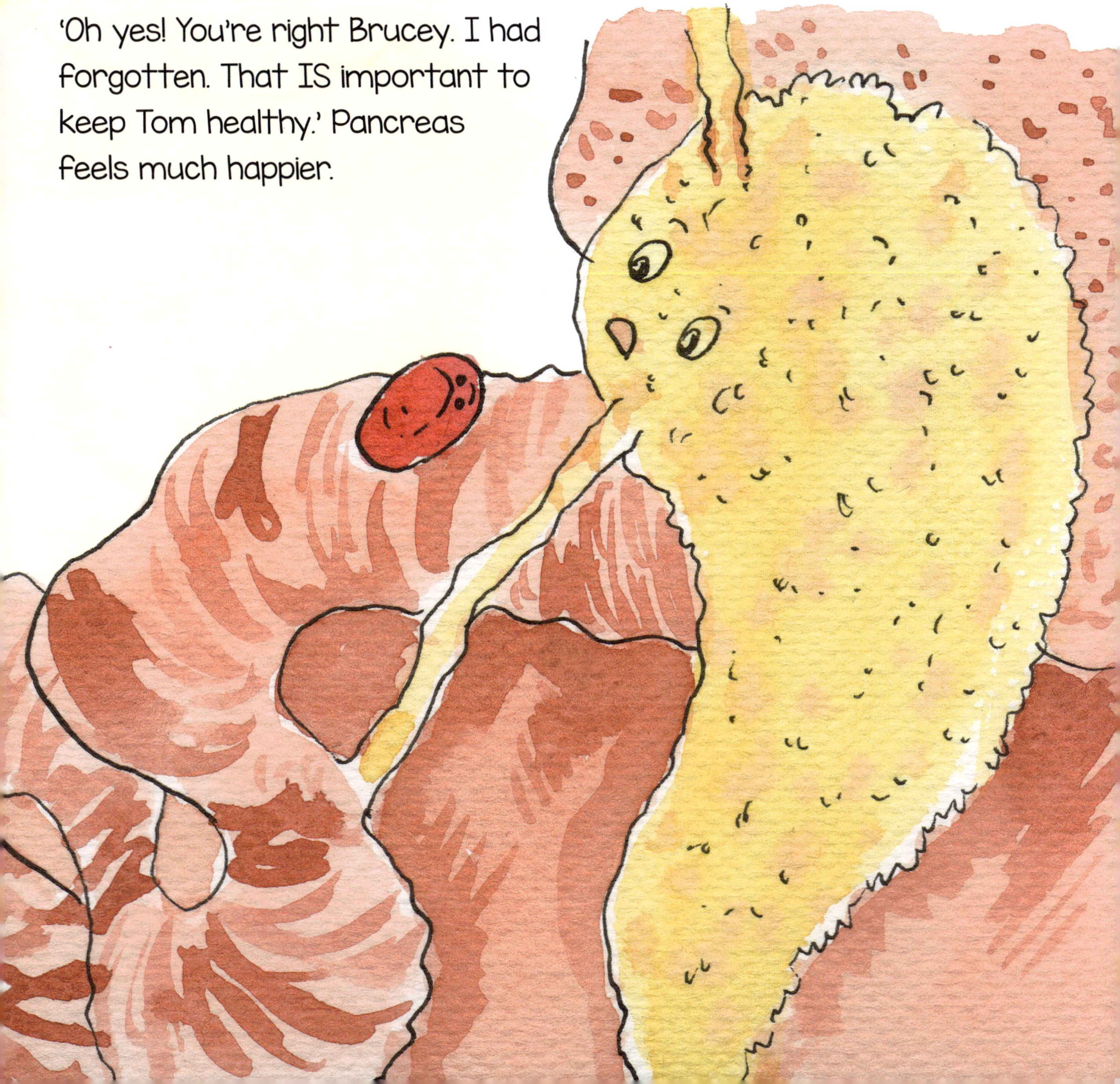

Tom and his Mum spend several days in the Children's Ward until he is eating and drinking normally again. He had to be careful what he ate and drank. When you have diabetes you have to make sure you eat a healthy diet and do not miss meals.

Tom wears a little box with the tube attached so that his body always has a supply of insulin. Robert comes to visit him and they have a GREAT time playing with the toys on the ward! Robert says: 'I hope you come home soon. I miss playing with you.'

CHAPTER 6

Back home...

It isn't long before Tom is allowed home. The first thing he does is to ask Robert around to play. Tom wants to show him his special insulin box and tube. Robert screws his face up.
'Blimey Tom, do you have to have that all the time no matter where you are?'

Tom grins.

'I have got used to it now Robert. I forget it's there most of the time and it keeps me feeling well so we can play together.' Robert smiles. He can't wait to show Tom his new tractor.
'I was so upset when I found out you were ill, I decided to keep my new tractor in its box until you came home from hospital.'

Together they open the box to reveal a large green and yellow tractor plus loads of other things to fit on the back, like a plough, a trailer and a seed drill.

'Wow, fantastic!' says Tom.

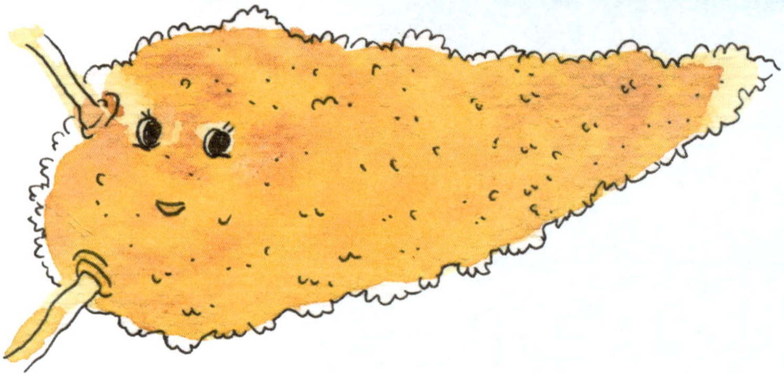

Every day Tom checks his insulin pump and needle with Mum's help. The food he eats still turns into glucose. The insulin from the pump unlocks the CELLS for the glucose like Susie and her friends. Mum helps Tom check how much glucose is in Brucey Blood, they decide what activities he will be doing and then they set the pump to give the right amount of insulin.

Sometimes, when Tom eats a lot more than usual or has a lot of sugary things, Brucey Blood gets cross. 'He's eating too much and there isn't enough insulin to open the CELLS for it all,' he grumbles.

When Mum and Tom do the glucose test and see Brucey has too much, they adjust the insulin being delivered from the pump.

At Easter time Tom complains to Mum that it is unfair that he can't have all his chocolate eggs at once. She knows that if he eats them too quickly he will be ill! Tom knows Mum is right really and says he is sorry, giving her a hug.

Tom finds that if he uses up a lot of energy running around or going swimming but doesn't eat enough, he feels unwell. If he catches a cold or is poorly with something like chickenpox, Mum has to keep a close watch on his blood glucose levels too. Being poorly can make the levels higher or lower than usual.

Learning to manage Tom's diabetes takes quite a while but with the help of the doctors and nurses at the hospital, his parents, friends and Miss Pigglebottom all learn about it so that they can help him.

Robert helps Tom as much as he can. When he notices Tom looking unwell he checks to see whether he needs something to eat or if he has remembered to check his insulin pump. Robert doesn't mind helping Tom with his diabetes; he is just so happy that Tom is back kicking the ball, playing with the tractor and best of all, is able to be his mate in this year's Three Legged Race!

Where has Susie been?

1 FOOD PIPE (OESOPHAGUS)

2 PANCREAS

3 SMALL INTESTINE AND VILLI

4 BLADDER

SUSIE SLIDING DOWN INTO THE STOMACH

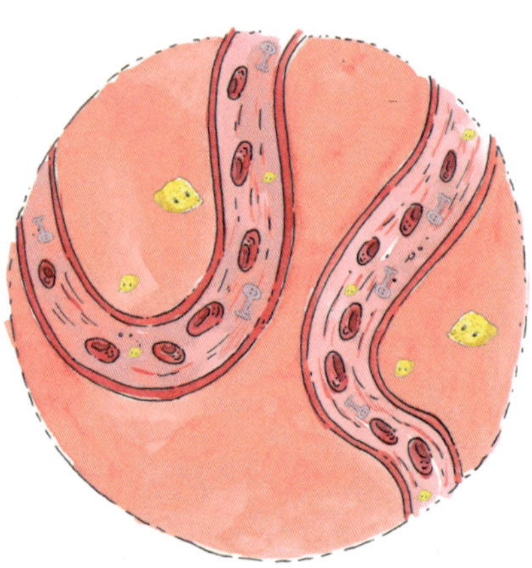

SUSIE MEETING BRUCEY AND INSULIN IN THE BLOOD VESSEL

SUSIE AND THE CELL

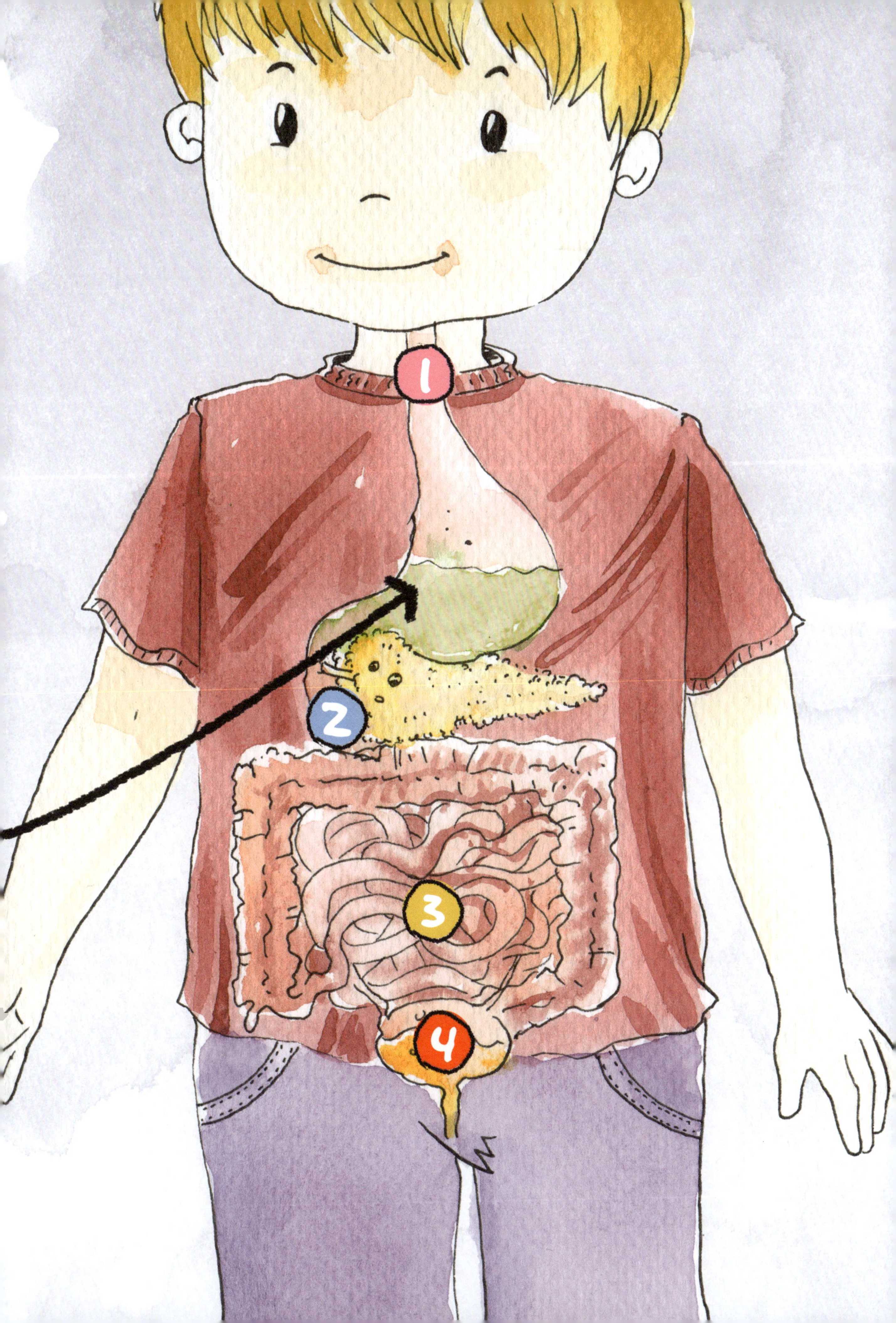
1
2
3
4

What does it all mean?

Blood is the red liquid that flows around the inside of your body and you can see it if you cut yourself. It flows like a river through tiny elastic tubes (known as vessels) around your body pumped along by the heart. It takes things like the air that we breathe and the food that we eat to different parts of the body to help keep us alive. It also plays an important role in protecting us against infection.

Cells these are very tiny. They are the smallest part of a plant or animal, each one containing millions of cells. The human body contains billions of these and are essential to perform the complex tasks necessary for life.

Cereals These are made from grain. Examples of these are wheat, corn or rice. It is used in breakfast cereal.

Diabetes (mellitus) is a condition in which the body does not produce enough insulin to be able to control the level of glucose in the blood.

Energy one example is the body having the strength and power to do active things. Another is the way the eye converts light energy into electrical nerve impulses to make vision possible.

Fat one form is contained in foods such as meat, cheese, oil, butter and nuts. It contains important vitamins needed for the body to function. Fat is an important part of a healthy diet especially for little children as it is needed to develop the nervous system and brain correctly. It can be used for energy, to help keep you warm and to form body fat. Body fat lies beneath the skin and around some of the internal organs. Excess amounts of fat are stored under the skin in obesity.

Glucose is a type of sugar that gives you energy. Sugar is changed into glucose in the small intestine. It is naturally present in fruit. It is also produced during the digestive process of products like carbohydrates. It is carried to all the tissues in the body by the blood where it can be used for energy.

Hormones These are 'chemical messengers' which are transported by the blood to make certain parts of your body do something; for example insulin, which opens the cells so that the body can use glucose for energy.

Hospital is a place where sick or injured people are given medical or surgical treatment with specialized staff and equipment.

Insulin is a substance that most people produce naturally in their body. It controls the level of glucose in the blood and is essential in the process of glucose being absorbed into cells where it is converted into energy. It is made in the pancreas by a cluster of cells known as the 'Islets of Langerhans'. In diabetes the body does not produce enough insulin to control the level of glucose in the body. It is one of many types of hormones in the body.

Islets of Langerhans see pancreas and insulin.

Ketones These are produced when the body starts using fat instead of carbohydrates for energy. If your blood glucose is normal and you are losing weight, it can be normal to have ketones sometimes. High levels can be found in diabetes when the body cannot use glucose normally. When they are found in the urine this is known as ketonuria.

Laboratory a room or building where special equipment is kept to test things, or do experiments.

Microscope these are used to make very small things look bigger so that more detail can be seen.

Muscle There are three types:

1. Skeletal muscle is a piece of tissue inside your body which is connected to your bones by tendons and gives your body shape. You use these muscles to make your body move.
2. Smooth muscles are in the walls of internal organs for example the intestine (peristalsis action which moves the food along); blood vessels; and the bladder.
3. Cardiac muscle which helps keep the heart beating thousands of times a day.

Organ a part of your body that has a particular type of function for example your heart or the pancreas.

Pancreas A large long organ in your body that can be found behind your stomach. A tiny part of it called Islets of Langerhans makes insulin. This is used to regulate the level of glucose in the blood. The pancreas also makes digestive juices. These juices mix with your food in the small intestine before the food can then be used in various parts of the body.

Small Intestine is the first and longest part of the intestine. It is in 3 parts - the duodenum, jejunum, and ileum. Here bile and enzymes are mixed with the food to help break it up into tiny bits. This is where most of the important things in your food is digested and then taken (by the blood for example) to where it is needed in your body.

Stomach This is a bit like a sack and is between the oesophagus and the small intestine. Food is mixed together here with liquid known as gastric juices (the big yellow pool) and partly digested before it moves into the small intestine.

Sugar is a sweet substance that is used to make food and drinks sweet. It can be found naturally in food such as apples and grapes. When you eat them, the body converts them into glucose and then it is used for energy. Too much can be bad for your body for example it can make you feel tired and rot your teeth.

Urine also known as pee. This is the pale yellow liquid that comes from the kidneys after cleaning the blood. It is kept in the bladder until you are ready to have a pee. Then it travels down the urethra and into a nappy or toilet for example.

Villi are soft tiny finger-like things that are on the inside walls of the small intestine. They provide a large surface area for the absorption of tiny bits of food from the intestine into the blood stream.

Ward this is a room in a hospital that usually has beds in it. It is used for people to have special medical treatments.

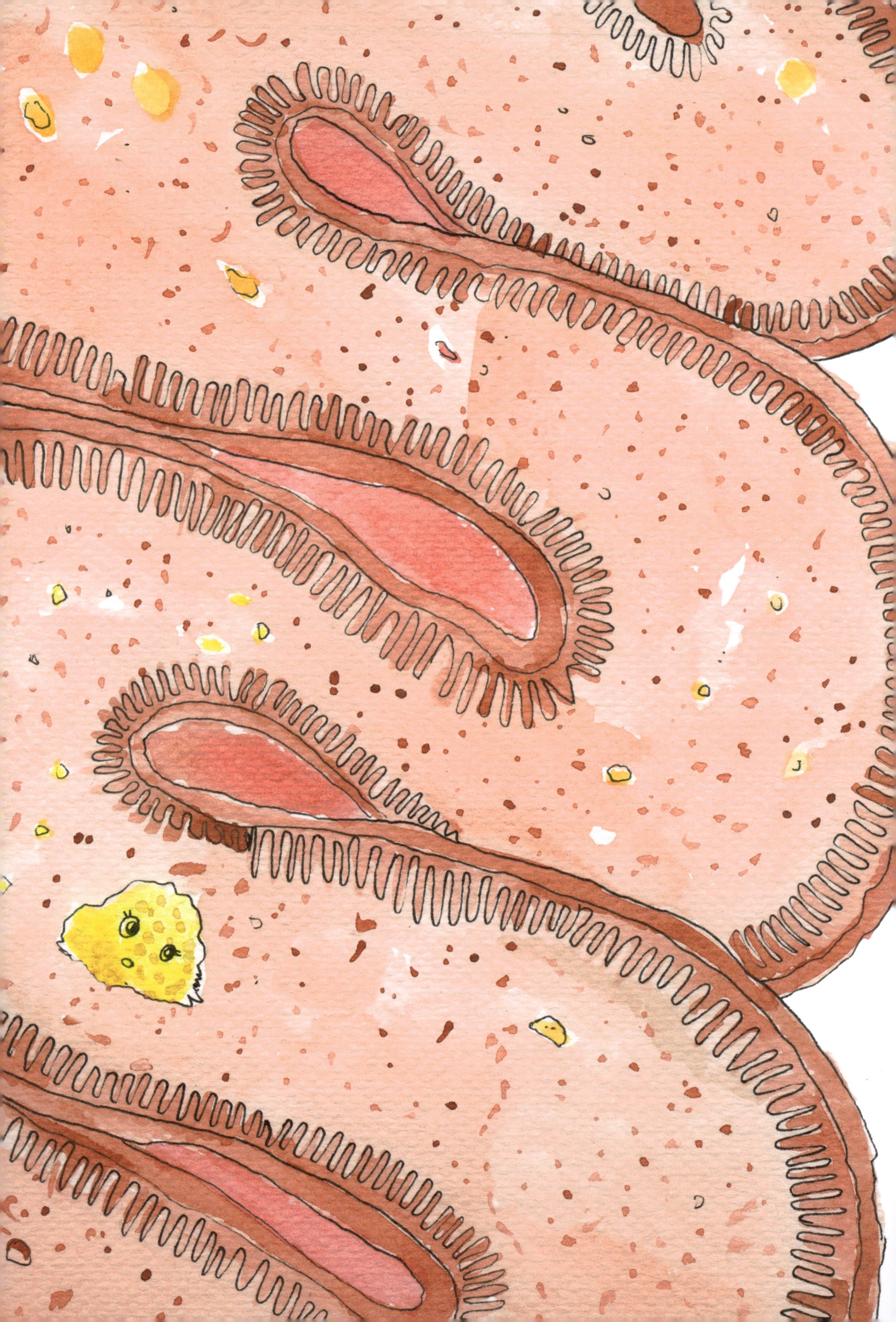

SUSIE SUGAR WORDSEARCH

H	S	C	L	S	M	A	S	H	C	D	E	R	N	Y
E	S	O	C	U	L	G	J	C	I	E	A	C	G	S
O	E	P	J	G	G	Q	Y	A	R	Q	L	R	O	Z
F	H	F	Q	A	P	I	B	M	V	T	E	L	R	F
Z	E	A	L	R	Z	E	M	O	J	N	P	U	S	L
U	V	P	X	A	T	O	G	T	E	R	R	S	W	Y
S	O	A	H	E	N	S	N	S	A	T	L	C	F	W
F	B	N	S	O	T	I	C	E	I	N	H	M	E	Z
B	X	C	U	A	S	V	L	V	F	G	K	J	T	J
I	E	R	A	Z	J	P	I	U	M	W	F	Q	E	R
M	B	E	J	W	B	L	I	F	S	N	R	T	A	Y
G	U	A	Y	E	L	T	D	T	N	N	V	A	X	U
U	G	S	Y	I	G	L	D	B	A	E	I	I	W	X
M	I	C	R	O	S	C	O	P	E	L	S	W	Z	P
T	N	W	B	L	O	O	D	M	S	D	Y	Y	R	K

BLOOD	CELLS	DIABETES
ENERGY	GLUCOSE	HOSPITAL
INSULIN	MICROSCOPE	PANCREAS
STOMACH	SUGAR	VILLI

Other Books by... The BUSY BODY Series

Suitable for key stage 1 & 2

Written By Heather Hawley
Illustrated by Sarah-Leigh Wills

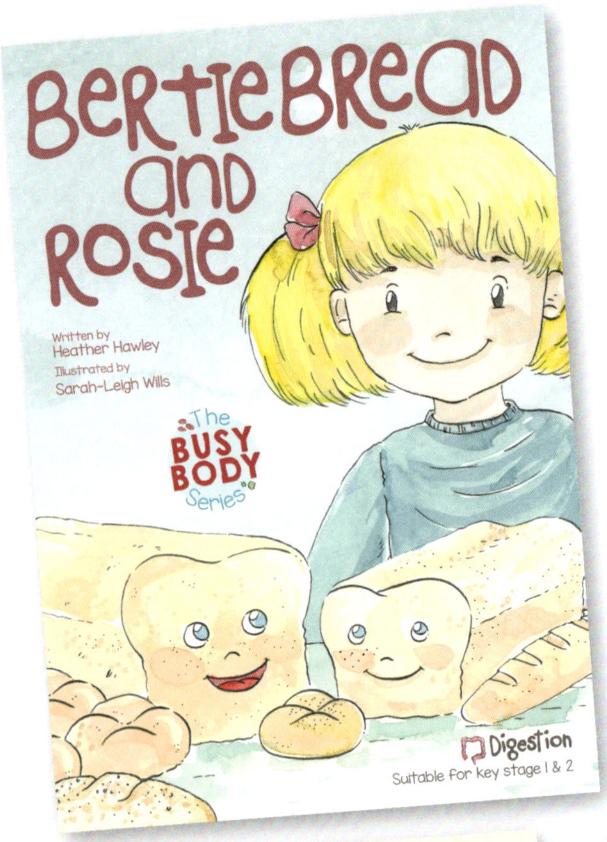

about...

Digestion...

Bertie Breads adventures through Rosie's body are used to explain the process of food from the mouth to the toilet. He meets up with Brucey Blood who explains how bread is used to keep Rosie strong and healthy. The Gas Family and bacteria are used to help illustrate why at times you feel 'windy' during digestion!

ISBN 978-0-9931014-0-3

£6.99

about...

Kidneys and renal system....

The adventures of Josie Juice through Matthew's body are used to explain what happens to the fluid in our bodies. She meets up with Brucey Blood who explains how the water she is made of is important to Matthew. The journey starts as a glass of juice, which travels from the small intestine, through the renal artery to the kidneys, eventually being passed as urine. It even explains why Matthew ended up with a wet patch in his pants when he wanted to stay with his friends rather than go to the toilet!

ISBN 978-0-9931014-2-7

£6.99

The Author Heather...

"I have worked as an Advanced Nurse Practitioner (BSc (Hons) ACNP) in a GP surgery since 1999 and many of the patients I see are children. Working with children in the medical field can be challenging. Sometimes a creative imagination is useful in order to gain their confidence; this can help the children and their parents to understand the condition and the medical interventions we are making. With this in mind I decided to write the Busy Body Series."

The illustrator Sarah...

"My style of illustration has regularly been referred to as fun and inventive, the 'quirky designer' being a nickname I have regularly heard. My focus is now on childrens books, 98% of my work these days is just that, and I couldnt think of anything better, a complete excuse for me NOT to let my mind grow up!! I love creating educational books for children, in fact its now a passion of mine, helping them understand through my illustrations. ... and I LOVE music & Haribo!"

Find out more at: www.busybodyseries.co.uk